It Was Over Before It Started

Gary J. Nash

PAGE PUBLISHING
Conneaut Lake, PA

First originally published by Page Publishing 2023

ISBN 978-1-6624-6123-1 (pbk)
ISBN 978-1-6624-6124-8 (digital)

Printed in the United States of America

Contents

Introduction

This is about a young Black man like those who have come from a poor environment with hardworking parents and who come from poor roots. This book is about the survival of all obstacles in life and how to succeed. I thank God and all the significant people who played a part in my accomplishment. Any person could write a story about his life, but what really inspired me to write this book was I had minor learning disabilities when I was a kid. Also, life was or seemed to be always difficult and a struggle at times. I just wanted to let the significant people in my life know how I felt about everything or situation that I encountered. I want to let them know that I love them all.

Chapter 1

Personal Upbringing

My story began on November 10, 1961, in Dallas, Texas, when I was born at Parkland Memorial Hospital—the same place John F. Kennedy passed away. My parents are Gladys Pearl Woolen Nash and Theo Nash, and my grandparents are Effie Mae Jackson Woolen and Richard Joe Woolen. My grandparents on my father's side are Debron Nash and Zoria Marshall Nash. They made their living as farmers, working at lumberyard. My mother and father worked as educators in Dallas Independent School System to raise me and my five other siblings—three boys and two girls. My dad came from small town in East Texas named Gilmer, and my mother came from a small town named Elysian Fields, Texas, outside of Marshall, Texas. They met at Bishop College, now presently located in Dallas. After graduation, they moved to South Dallas from Marshall, Texas, at 3505 Myers Street at the corner of Grand Avenue. After I was born in November 1961, we moved to 3714 Tioga Street, Oak Cliff, Dallas, with my oldest brother, Kenneth. I was mostly babysat by my aunts and uncles until I was able to attend school while my mom and dad worked and continued their education to keep the new home. I watched my parents work hard to better themselves, to earn more money, and to get the necessary things we needed. I was not a very good student in school due to disfunctions at home. Attending school was a very hard adjustment due to depression at young age; my grades were very poor.

I had problems keeping up with the other kids. Bringing home reports with Ds and Fs caused me even more problems at home. So that was my young life up until sixth grade. I started middle school at John F. Kennedy in seventh and eighth grades. I experienced trying to find myself on what I wanted to do—trying out for the basketball team—and getting release was not good enough. I always enjoyed all sports as a kid. Also, I experienced some bullying, not much, but was very intimidated by this because I was trying to find out what kind of person I was at home and in school. I got through those two years and went on to ninth grade, freshman year, at Wilmer-Hutchins High School. In all those four years, I could say it was a new experience. Being on campus with older kids was a big adjustment in 1976, but I got through again. My grades were not very good but below average. I had given up on any chances of playing sports or any other activities due to depression and drug use at home and in school.

My tenth grade sophomore year started; it was time to get a job and become more responsible so I could supply my own school items. This was the tone of things around the house. At age sixteen, my junior year started. I experienced sex and experimented on marijuana and alcohol just to feel normal. It caused me more depression but overall considered myself functional, trying to finish high school while living in a dysfunctional family. I continued to attend school and work different types of jobs to help out the household. I managed to reach the twelfth grade by attending half a day and the other half going to American Trade School. But unfortunately, in year the 1979, just before the graduation, a severe tornado tore through the school and damaged the campus; no students ever returned to the school. From there, everyone moved to Bishop College campus which is known today as Paul Quinn College to obtain their high school diploma.

Mother always made sure we attended church on Sunday. We were encouraged to attend and become a member of Mount Tabor Baptist Church; Reverends Harris and Nash were the pastors at that time.

I never committed to one main girlfriend in high school. I had a lot of girls interested in me. But I chose to use alcohol and drugs than have sex with girls. The only girl I had sex several times was Betty Clark, the neighborhood girl across the street. She was my first sexual intercourse at age sixteen. I could say that my life had just begun. I made an attempt to attend college at Cedar Valley Community College due to my poor grades and effort in high school. In my first semester, I only took twelve hours and dropped every class. But I gradually got the hang of college life and what I needed to do to be successful. It was totally different from high school. My good friend, Dwayne Fitzgerald, and I attended college and helped each other get through. We continued until we finished on July 1, 1982, and graduated with an Associate Degree In Arts and Science. On July 15, 1982, I joined the US Air Force at age twenty-one and was discharged on December 14, 1982, from active duty. I became an Active Reserve and had weekend duty until July 14, 1985.

I was discharged because of a negative urinalysis which ended my military career with an Honorable Discharge. I continued to suffer with addiction to marijuana use and alcohol. I always knew I wanted to be somebody, finishing junior college and entering into military. Drugs and alcohol continued to be apart of my life. But now I came with the task of finding a professional job to support myself and my family. I got myself a job with the Greyhound Trailways Bus Company. I worked there for about three years until I felt driving wasn't for me. I continued to try to live on my own; there were a number of other jobs thereafter. Finally, in the year 1991, after my lower back surgery in 1988, I met an older woman named Patricia Roy, who became my common law wife from 1991 to January 2005. That was when the ideas came to me in writing old sayings and street poetry about my thoughts and feelings daily. Mostly, the life of a Black man on how life is supposed to be. I had to start my first chapter about recovery due to my consistent problems with drugs and alcohol use as a teen.

The steps of my journey were leaving home at the age of twenty-one in year 1982 to join the United States Air Force Reserve and having a two-year college degree from Cedar-Valley Community College. It was a major change in my life, suffering from depression, addiction to drugs and alcohol, and other street drugs. Having to go cold turkey to get off of drugs was a hard task. But the change in environment helped. After about six months, I felt like a new person. Praise be to God! My bad habits were gone. My life really began when I learned about the recovery on October 14, 1999. I began trying to stay off the use of drinking alcohol and smoking marijuana by getting a job in a substance abuse treatment facility named Cornell Correction in Wilmer, Texas. It's your choice on what life has to offer. During this time in my life, I turned to trying to help others as I was helped.

I finally realized that we can't save everybody and some people don't want to be saved. The most important people who played a major role in our future and in becoming a productive adult are our family and parents. This structure is a foundation for learning values, responsibility, and goals. A young person mirrors his parents' behavior while growing up. Next would be the pastor of a church who teaches us to surrender and turn our lives over to God completely. Other role models would be a teacher, coach, or counselor, who we encounter frequently for 365 days in a school year, help us find a path to take in life. These professionals confront positive and negative behavior and console grief issues and concerns that we may have at home or school until we graduate and become part of the world. Therapeutic environment is a foundation for change, learning the person to reflect on life and make necessary changes to accomplish goals and become well again. Mentoring process is an excellent model in helping a person not to make mistakes, continue to grow, and have a support system. It also gives young people an opportunity to make the right choices in life. This can cause less mistakes and more positive outlook. A lot of becoming successful can be contributed to these different processes.

Here are a few thoughts: Life is what you make it. Easy come, easy go. Sometimes being right isn't enough, that's why I feel those people who do wrongs. More old sayings, I either heard growing up or experienced it personally. I might be a fool today, but this doesn't mean I'll be a fool tomorrow. The way a person views his life is in the eyes of the beholder or themselves. You are damned if you do, and you are damned if you don't. If anything good comes out of a given situation, it should not be looked upon as sad. Other old sayings: Wherever there is a beginning, there will be an end. Two wrongs don't make a right; it just means you are dishonest or a cheat. Thought of the day: There are some decisions that you have to make for yourself. The three top choices you have to make at some point in your life to be successful are educational choices, the relationships you choose, and the career you choose to make a living to support yourself and family.

Thought of the day, June 24, 2003: Wise people say you have to be a follower before you can lead. Some say you have to be taught first before you can learn. My theory is our overall experience is our best teacher. A perfect person would say, "Why become follower when you can lead or be a leader?" The bottom line is, learn the lesson before you can teach a lesson. Personal thoughts for today at 9:10 a.m.: I'm not feeling very happy with my personal relationship, making long-term commitments, as well as in my professional life. Sometimes I wanted to be married and find peace in myself and a career that is not stressful and gives me the type of pay I deserve. As I grew older in life, I wanted someone to love and show me love daily. I felt this would make me a better person and I would commit and honor God's word. The personal thought for that day was arrange business papers to get better organize for a better tomorrow. I was hoping to work for myself or get a better-paying job and was hoping to get back into church soon.

Today, I woke up, sitting around and thinking of my upcoming court date with my attorney to receive my Social Security disability benefits. I was very hopeful that I would win and I could continue with the positive progress in my life. At age fifty-six and soon to be fifty-seven on November 10, which was on a Saturday in 2018, I wanted to talk about a few disappointments as I reached this older age and not having any children and the two women who supposed to have been pregnant by me, not wanting to take responsibility of giving birth.

Today was another day. On October 5, 2018, I got a text from high school class of 1979 to attend the homecoming celebration. I decided not to attend the homecoming event because I wanted to focus more on my future than focusing on my past. I wished everyone to enjoy themselves, be safe, and have a good time maybe next year. Here is a list of my deceased classmates from the class of 1979 of Wilmer Hutchins: (1) Dwayne Fitzgerald, (2) Joe Lynn, (3) Timothy Harris, (4) Jimmy Parnell, (5) Marlo Fowler, (6) Earl Lankford, (7) Randell Haynes, (8) Michael Pierce, (9) Kevin Thompson, (10) Kelvin Jackson, (11) Vicky Bradford, (12) Subrina Stubblefield, (13) Lester Frazier, (14) Grace Echo, (15) Mercedes Dawson, (16) Patricia Deckard, (17) Michelle Brown, (18) Jarriet Bell, (19) Charlene Chiles, (20) James McDaniels, (21) Reginald Hamilton, (22) Danny Hampton, (23) Yvonne Curtis, (24) Junita Rhoades, (25) Lamont Rand, (26)Alan Moss, (27) Reginald Carrin, (28) Gloria Perkins, (29) Sandy Candey, (30) Don Jones, (31) Clifford Salser, and (32) Cynthia Wills. These were up to date as of March 23, 2020. Back to class of 1979, graduates currently continued to live on this date. On April 7, 2019, I got a text to have a short meeting with some of the classmates to prepare for the fortieth year class reunion at Spring Creek Barbeque on Wheatland Road. I stayed only for about two hours, waiting for people to show up; only about fifteen people showed up. Some came to be in good health, a few came to be just holding on, not in such good health, but remember, this was our fortieth year reunion planning. I never realized there were a total of 650 classmates in 1979. The date set for the reunion was September 2019.

I had not written anything in awhile, while experiencing a lot of grief issues. More loved ones have passed on, but life still feels okay. The struggle continues on but still very hopeful about the future. On my fifty-sixth birthday, I had never experienced the effects of an enlarged prostate. It was very painful and uncomfortable feeling. My efforts to handle this disease will be a day by day, one day at a time struggle.

Chapter 2

Ups and Downs of a Boy to Becoming a Man

A few good books for you to read as your life comes together to feel complete and become a better person and be more knowledgeable with your culture and environment are *Katrina Brownlee's Journey: From Rock Bottom to Success in Unlikely Place*; *The Promise Land*, author Barrack Obama; *Will*, author Will Smith; *Comfortable Conversation with Blackman*, author Acho Emmanel; *Longtime Coming*, author Dr. Eric Michael Dyson; *On Juneteeth*, author Annette Gordan Reed; *Black in Blue*, author Carmen Best; and *Blessing in Broken Places*, author Mel Jackson.

The thought for the day was there is such thing as burning a bridge with a person that you can never cross again. The Ten Commandments are very important rules of life for living a life of righteousness and integrity for young person to live by as a guide. It becomes a time when we have to be accountable for our problems. There comes a time that we have to stop using profane language to express ourselves. It is not how you play the game; it is knowing the rules of the game, and that is when you can master the game and play it well. These are thoughts a few months after Patricia passed away on June 14, 2006. Roses are red. Violets are blue. Today I love you. White rose is pureness, like the wind, snow, rain, and a sunny day. Yellow rose is like a beautiful friendship that needs to shine like the sun. Different species that roam the earth like animals and wildlife, birds, and fish are creations for us as humans to enjoy as a gift from God. Love never dies. People do. So just give me away my heart, soul, and all of me. Love is a good thing but can be abused. Love is blind, but can be a good thing for the heart. Love is what we all need and crave as human beings. Love is happiness, and love is sad. I truly believe it is okay to love someone, something, but never stop loving yourself and what you stand for. When something is already done, it is spilled milk under a bridge. It means to clean your mess up or straight up. If you are really thirsty, you must refill the glass. It means to move on to the next chapter of your life. If you let someone go or something, it should come back. It is always good to let go of someone, to see if the feelings are strong enough to recreate the spark. Feeling optimistic about the future, the sky is limit. We can't turn back time; we can only go forward into the future. It is not where you come from, it ultimately comes down to where you are going.

I firmly believe that a person should build bridges, not burn bridges. Another way of saying this is build relationships, not destroy them. We as men can't live without women, and we sure can't live totally without a woman. There is always an end and a new beginning. Every man for himself and God for us all. We never know what we have until it's gone; it means that people are special. My major theory of how the world works is people are in control of power. Overall this is God's world and all the things in it he created, from people to animals, nature, and natural destruction. I've seen many people passed away year after year, and the world just keeps on going. More people are born and more people die. Natural disaster continues to happen year after year, and all we can do as humans is repair, prepare, and rebuild. Today, I am thinking about my life as I live out the last years of it. I felt depression most times but always knew I was gifted person with hidden skills. To be able-minded to do whatever and accomplish my goals. At this point, I feel am behind in the game of life at least ten years. What I know as a sixty-year-old, I should have known as a fifty-year-old. Getting older is always a good thing, being able to enjoy the wisdom, fame, and money that comes with it all. God gives and God takes away.

The path I took might not work for everyone, but so far it had worked for me. I always had interest in becoming a homeowner, and I did at age thirty-four, which is late for most people. I started out renting in November 1997, nine months after my father passed away. I had lived in that home for about twenty years. A goal I didn't think I could accomplish. More young people need to experience of what it means to pay a mortgage versus renting. The word *mortgage* has a history, meaning "paid in full," with the word *gage* meaning "until death." We are born, we live, then we die. On March 28, 2019, I got good news from my attorney; I was officially retired because of chronic low back condition. It was another step toward my final journey, till death do us part. If I could only start over and redo my life, I would not have chosen the path or choices I made. Life is a learning experience; you have to involve yourself to know what is right for you professionally as well as personally. Nevertheless, I can't change much how I am 58 years of age, it is about trying to keep faith and survive.

Personal thoughts for today: I had a good day off from work; I was just resting around house. I got a call from a couple of old friends from the neighborhood—Steve Richardson and Howard Bolden. I also bumped into friends at work from the old neighborhood—Larry Young, Ray Shannon, Keith Young, Stacey McGregor, Larry Range. We all attended the same schools. I also wanted to mention a couple of good friends' upcoming birthdays, Steve R. March 31, James E, October 31, Joel C, October 28, Herman G. August 10. We all grew up together during our younger years from age six to fifteen. At this age now, it felt good to see how for we all have come every time I ran across high school friends as well grade school. On November 2, 2018, it was another day just like any other; I bumped into another neighbor from my new neighborhood where I currently resided— Mrs. Jane, the old Caucasian lady working at the Dollar General store. The reason I was mentioning this is she lived right at the back of my house for years until her husband got sick and passed away; she also lost her home. I was a very young man at that time, I just moved in to the neighborhood.

The story was my impression of her was she seemed to be racist, but to make long story short, she was just the opposite; she planted a garden in the backyard and gave me lots of tomatoes. She was a lot older and friendly and became a very good neighbor; it was just good to see she was still living. Also I just wanted to mention another very good friend, Carolyn, a Caucasian lady, fifty-eight, one of my best friends. We currently continue to call each other from time to time. Also I wanted to mention Michael, another good friend; I met him as I worked in my career as a juvenile detention officer back in 2006. He was from Kansas City, Missouri, and I had recently spoke with him. He was doing okay but had some health problems with His kidneys; he was on dialysis at age sixty-three. As my life gets closer to the end, good friends are hard to find—another one of my old sayings.

I talked to my oldest sister and brother; she had news about one of my cousins on my father side of the family who had passed away. His name was Clanford Jr. he was sixty-six years old, keeping up to speed date. On April 6, 2020, two years later, I got more news of another family member's death; his brother, Jerry Lynn Nash, another cousin, died because of the current coronavirus spread. But that was no surprise at my age; somebody is leaving the world whether family or friends. I was just sitting around, drinking on a beer, having thoughts about life and my new habits—horse racing, playing the slot machines from time to time. Another day while shopping at Walmart when I bumped into cousin Sherry Margene, daughter at the Red Oak location. On another occasion, I saw my other cousin, Michell, at Walmart in Wheatland Road, Dallas. Also I had seen Michelle's husband Robert, and Tanita's husband, John, at the car auction in Wilmer, Texas. I did recognize my people when I ran across them daily. I wanted to talk about the family reunion on my mother's side. I had a very good time; people showed up from Oklahoma, California, and Texas. Everybody seemed to be doing well. People who attended were my aunts, cousins, nieces, nephews, uncles, brothers-in-law, sisters-in-law, friends, and many more. It was like old times, but instead of having the reunion in the countryside, we had it in the city. November 10, 2018, my birthday, it was another day as usual, waking up, getting ready to shower, and getting dressed to meet my brother and his wife for lunch at Hooters—a sports restaurant. Everything went well. Brother Kenneth also was there; we had good conversation. TVs were all over the place.

I got more news about my old grade school friend from my neighborhood; he passed away because of cancer. Herman Jr. was his name; his mother and father were good people. They lived about four houses up the block. It went back to my story; it was over before it started. All good things come to an end.

On February 8, 2019, the new year had begun starting out kind of slow, and I got an invitation to attend the sixtieth birthday celebration of my cousins, Cynthia Woolen and Scottie Allen. It was wintertime and slightly cold outside, about thirty degrees with windchill of twenty. The event went well with many important people.

Five reasons why I am always going to win and I truly believe this. (1) I don't hate anyone. (2) I pray. (3) I stay in my lane. (4) I don't try to compete with anyone. (5) I always stay humble. This is my theory on living a healthy good life.

On March 22, 2019, springtime began. I was just sitting, watching the daily news, and couldn't believe that people were involving themselves in such crazy behavior. Old saying, just a sign of the times. Life is changing for the worst; hopefully, something good will come out of it. Life laws change and so do people. A White man at the downtown area pulled a gun on a defenseless Black woman. Also a Black man punched a woman in the face for no good reason. We also had Black-on-Black crime when somebody just bumped your car and you got shot and killed over petty incidents. There was a Black woman going into a barbershop on Grand Avenue killing three Black men. These were just examples of the bold attacks on innocent people. Today was a new day, just lying in the bed, thinking on how I had come to this point in my life, experiencing more medical problems as I aged. And I would like to let the younger generation know that life is good and can get difficult at times. You must make a plan and stick to it. Life is like a race; it has a starting point and a stopping point. Get all you can out of life while you can. Life is like a car, running out of gas; you can refuel it or leave it empty.

I had another night of restless and irritation due to my prostate and was up and down, going to the bathroom, but was functioning okay. Another one of my old sayings is nothing comes to a sleeper but a dream. The key is to keep moving forward. A few days after Mother's Day, I got an invitation to attend my niece's graduation from college; her name is Daisha, the daughter of my brother, Anthony, and Janell. I couldn't attend but expressed to him how much this is a great moment for him and his wife to be proud of their accomplishment. I got more news that another childhood neighbor and friend, Clifford, had passed away. On April 17, 2020, another old friend had passed away. His name was Charles, age sixty-eight; he was the cook at the famous family chicken place called Halls Chicken. I would very much like to attend the funeral, but because of the coronavirus, the government was not letting people gather in groups. A sign of the times, hopeful about what tomorrow will bring.

On Sunday, April 19, 2020, I was just having a few thoughts; I wanted to share on how God give us a chance to surrender our life over to him whether good or bad. The reason I mentioned this is because I have seen this over, as I aged, people live the way they see fit. They may be successful or not, but they live good lives, they have families and friends. Nevertheless, it becomes a time when you must let God come in and surrender your life. It could be due to old age, chronic addiction, medical condition, or even if we feel life is just not exciting enough anymore. We have no choice but to leave our loved ones behind. I have to say that it's not a bad thing; it's just what we are born to do as human beings. Being blessed is not about having things or objects. It's about trusting in yourself and God's Word and being able to wake up another day. Enjoying the fresh air, taking a deep breath while taking in natural sunlight God has produced. We can get busy living or get busy dying; it's like a car, struck in neutral not going anywhere. It only takes a little will power to just keep driving or going in the right direction; that is my theory on how the way life is. Life could be similar to a chicken recipe; every place cooks it differently. There have been moments in my life; I must wonder the reason why I am still here. But I know the answer to that question. It's God's will; I can recall on at least three occasions. I had a gun in my face; I could have been shot but I survived. The first was on Bonnie View Road. I was just walking from neighborhood store. The second time was in South Dallas on South Boulevard near Fair Park. Third time was with a friend in South Dallas on Park Row, both times doing things, I should have not been doing.

The State Fair of Texas had started on September 27, 2019. Back to true facts about the way life really is, no matter what race you may be, we have to be completely accountable for ourselves for our success and downfalls in life. We walk around killers, evil people looking to do wrong daily. Not ever knowing when we might snap or just make a terrible decision we will regret for rest of our lives. On December 13, 2019, I got good news and some bad news. The good news was my brother Patrick's son, Xavier, was graduating college from the University of Houston with a bachelor of science degree. Now the bad news was my sister's husband, Steven Ates, passed away because of cancer; he was a good person, a hard worker and had a good family who made the Nash family become stronger. He was with Cassandra for twenty-seven years; Steven was born in Austin, Texas, on December 22, and he was fifty-four.

At this moment in my life, I wanted to continue to carry the load or release the load or just light the load to continue to live. Most people try to stay on the consistence path and stick on what they believe in the most. We all will fight the battle, but in the end, we will all come up short. On the twenty-first day of December, my sister, Cassandra Ates Nash, turned fifty-four years old. She had the biggest celebration that any one could want for her fifty-fourth birthday. All the relatives, friends from both sides of each family were present for the burial service. I really felt it was a true blessing; she got to enjoy her birthday with friends, family, and everyone she and Steve ever knew. On January 2, 2020, I was just sitting back, thinking about the future and what tomorrow might bring. It came over me that we can't ever predict what might happen in the future; we can only plan for the next day. Hoping we can reach our long term plans. Life is unpredictable and uncertain; we have to believe as humans that we don't know what tomorrow will bring. Old sayings one day at a time.

This is a good way to live and survive; don't stop planning because we just might reach our goals.

On January 3, 2020, Friday was going into Saturday morning. I was awake and couldn't sleep, thinking how crazy the world was and all the problems you could encounter along the way. But the only thing I could come up with that would make any sense was to enjoy a lovely day. At the end of the day, you will be going home to your family and loved ones, locking your doors and taking care of yourself daily. The world can make us feel disfunctional as we live from day to day. Life is a repetition, doing things over and over; but in the end, there is always some kind of reward.

G. Nash Home 3/2022

Patricia Roy Byrd
My Significant Lady 13 yrs.
1992 until 2005

Chapter 3

Past History to Current History
Old Sayings to Help Stay Focused Daily

On January 20, 2020, it was Martin Luther King national holiday—the beginning of a new year and a new decade. This brought to my attention to acknowledge more about Black History—the people who were honored before my existence to make this a better place. Doris Miller was a Black man in the Navy who fought in Pearl Harbor in 1941 from Waco, Texas. Famous guitarist, Gary Clark, from Austin, Texas, Eddie Bernice Johnson, a Black woman politician, were representing Blacks in Washington from Waco, Texas. Another was Catherine Johnson, a mathematic genius who worked with the NASA space program in Houston, Texas. These were some of the important things I started to appreciate at this point in my life as I continued my journey.

African American people play a very meaningful role in today's society. We all fall short of our goals and desire of what we want life to be. When I say this, I mean family, friends, having a place to belong, integrity, our accomplishments, and a lot more. Because at the end of the day, the battle will end and the journey will be over.

On January 24, 2020, it was my mother's birthday, the lady who gave birth to me; she would have been eighty years old that day. She is Gladys Pearl Woolen Nash. That day was a good day because we also celebrated our aunt Margie's birthday, and Aunt Daisy's birthday was on January 25. Also Aunt Mattie's birthday was the twenty-second of January, and another was Arnold's birth month, Mattie's brother. Also my brother, Kenneth Nash, turned sixty years of age on January 19. Knowledge and power runs the world, but God owns the world; this is his world. Today March 16, 2020 we had been going through a silent invisible war sense in October 2019; around this time, the world was normal and everything was running smooth.

We had been hearing about an unknown virus that had entered the United States; it was called coronavirus that came from China and killed thousands of people in that country. The United States and several other countries had been infected. The president at this time was Donald Trump. Many people here had been infected and didn't even know until people started dying from the flu-like symptom. Come to find out it was a new virus that attacks the lungs and affects the immune system and causes death. It started in China through contamination of food being processed. Some people did recover after being infected, but most died. This had caused the United States economy to close down. It caused lost jobs, and many people had been put on quarantine to stay in their homes unless they needed to retrieve food or gas or work essential jobs.

I would like to speak about some of the facts I have learned along my journey to the very end of life. These helpful tips may save you time or not waste your time. Also these may ease some heartache and pain or save money by making wise decision in becoming a successful person. Ultimately all good things come to an end. Another thought came over me about life: As a human being, we all are considered a young person during our adolescent years from ages one to eighteen. We are not knowledgeable about our decision making so we need guidance. I also believe that from eighteen to fifty years of age, we become fully true adults. As I look back, that gives us about thirty-two years before we reach fifty; this gives us time to enjoy what life has to offer before we become old and our body starts to fail us. We begin having all types of illness. It has been proven that we can live a good, strong, healthy life for twenty or thirty years after age fifty. It is a gift to get to be an older adult, but just looking back, life is not very long at all.

On May 3, 2020, one week away from Mother's Day, I got news from Valencia Nash McShann that more family members had passed away because of illness; Aunt Julia and Aunt Gwen; Theola's daughter; and brother of Larry fair uncle were already deceased. She left her one son, Xavier, behind; they resided in the Fort Worth, Texas, area. We also lost Uncle Arthur Ray's wife, Maxine, from Tenaha, Texas; she left behind her three children, Johnny Ray, Ray Junior, Janice, and grandchildren.

Like I said, early life is like a struggle; and once you get over the struggle, it becomes a battle to continue to live life and then we go home to be with God. It is never easy, living with the pain of losing loved ones over and over again and trying to maintain sense of overcoming the struggles of life. But in the end, we get to go home and rest in peace; after we die, we say job well done and the battle is over. Death always leave people with some grief and sadness each and every time, depending on the relationship of the person. There has been many times that God has sent angels into my life at times when I really needed a friend. A lady named Jeanetta from the city of Denver came to Dallas, and we became good friends just out doing my cd's and movie business. At that time, I had pending legal issues; she gave me a job, helping her out, running errors for her as a transporter. This was back in the year 2013 for about six months.

On May 18, 2020, people were starting to go back to work, and schools were holding graduations. The state of Texas was easing up on 100 percent quarantine at home and starting to let people open up business again to save the economy. The virus had killed about one hundred thousand people in the United States since we discovered the problem in early March 2020. On May 28, 2020, five years had already passed since my mom passed away in 2015. Hundreds and thousands of people had died because of the coronavirus outbreak. The unemployment rate was at the highest level since the great depression was at 13 percent, and people continued to lose jobs as small businesses closed.

On Tuesday, May 26, 2020, another Black man, by the name of George Floyd, was killed by a White police officer in the city of Minneapolis, Minnesota. This had caused riots and many protests around the country. The movement is called Black Lives Matter; it had caused destruction of businesses, being burned down in the city of Minneapolis and many other cities across the United States. This came at a stressful time because most people of all colors were fighting the spread of the coronavirus. For the first time in history since Martin Luther King riot for peace and injustice, people of all ethnic groups White, Black, Hispanic, Asian, and all immigrant marched together for the same cause. Year 2020 was a new decade, but problems continued to happen because of poor police training, policies, and practices. The African American community became victims in police killings and undercover hate groups. I would like to speak on a piece of Black history; I never learned about it in high school or college. The Greenwood District, Tulsa Oklahoma, was a community of wealthy Black people because of the discovery of oil in 1921; as I write and talked about this today, they say no one has been held accountable for the killings. During this time, they said they were not accountable for the killings of about three hundred Black people whose homes and businesses were burned to the ground due to not giving a Black man a fair jury trial for the rape of a White woman. The Black Lives Matter movement is alive and well with all the ethnic groups, rioting around the country for new police policy and other racial injustice. Today was a step in the right direction for the people to be as one because my time was ending before it even started.

On the Fourth of July, Independence Day 2020, I was just starting my day thinking that life is never exciting enough unless we are doing things we never experience or done before. Life can be very boring and repetitive when you as a person will feel at times that you are not so important even if you exist. With all of what's going on around us and me fighting daily with prostate cancer, I am just trying to live a normal life, day and night. People are now being asked to wear face covering out in public daily to keep the spread of the coronavirus in control. I am very thankful to be here for another day and will continue to try to reach my goals to fulfill a complete and meaningful life.

On July 12, 2020, Sunday, cousin Russell and his new wife, Ronni, were married at Bella Woods Wedding Chapel site in

Midlothian, Texas. It was very quick, but everyone enjoyed themselves and had a good time. We as people have to realize that people get old and stuff gets old. We have to make the best of what we are given and what we can accomplish in life. We sometimes have to fall before we get back up. That is the way we learn how not to fall again and not making those same mistakes. We come to see as time goes on, we work hard to provide for future generation to come. This is my outlook and experience for the sixty years of life I have lived. Stay positive and not having to redo everything, making a future for the next generation of young people. Because in the long run, feeling comfortable with our accomplishments knowing when the end of life is near. We should feel complete. We as people assume we become a burden and unloved in the world. I say just enjoy the moment and time we spend together as family, friends, and significant others.

On July 18, 2020, civil rights leader and Congressman John Lewis passed away at eighty years old because of cancer complication. His good friend, C. T. Vivian, who stood beside him during those tough years, also passed away at age ninety-five on the same day fighting for voting rights for Black Americans. Another historical moment today in Grand Prairie, Texas, was native Delmas Morton was allowed to go to elementary school in the district but was denied the right to attend in Grand Prairie High School because of desegregation in school policy. He later became a teacher and principal for thirty years in that same school district. He will be awarded a school, which will be named after him, for the wrong that was put upon him when he was a kid. This shows how wrongs can be made right and hard work pays off in the long run.

On July 24, 2020, baseball was going to continue its season. Also the finial few games of the NBA finished their 2020 season in a stadium called the bubble in Orlando, Florida. The playoff was played there as well. Family reunion 2020 was held this month and the Nash side was held on Zoom video web. I didn't attend. I didn't think it would be any fun for me.

The Navy had trained its first female African American fighter pilot, Lt. Madeline Swegle. As of August 1, 2020, over 150,000 people in the United States had been killed because of the coronavirus since March 15, 2020; no cure had been discovered at that time. On August 7, 2020, Friday, the Woolen Jackson reunion was held that weekend and I didn't attend because of video coverage. I didn't feel it would be any fun for me because of the pandemic, which continued to spread killing people. On a good note, news came that a local hero named Andre Emmett, a professional NBA star, was honored with an outside court, named in his behalf due to his tragic death, located at the YMCA facility in Oak Cliff on Ledbetter Drive. Mr. Emmett was a local Dallas Carter High School graduate.

Life can take a lot of twist and turns, but whatever path a person chooses, it has to be right for him. No one expects to deal with life's ups and downs all alone, but it's what you make of it and keep trying. My advice to the younger generation is to make wise choices because the wrong choice could cost you a lot of unnecessary time and heartache. I have continued to write about my life year after year; it's been repetitious for the most part. But from time to time, there will be something new that happens to talk about. Life continues to change more by the day, minute, year. We just have to keep living to see what tomorrow will bring. Thinking on all the new technology that has come about sense high school 1975 to 1979. We don't have cell phones, computers, Facebook, Instagram, Uber, the World Wide Web, Google, DNA testing, and smart television growing up. I have had to open my eyes to a new technology world, and it continues as I write my manual script of my life as I know it. My old saying is there is an easy way to die and an easy way to make a dollar.

On August 19, 2020, kids were officially returning to school either online learning or in person. Also the democrat national convention nominee for president was held during the last four days. Joe Biden and Kamala Harris, the first Black woman of color, had entered the race as vice president democrat party. The plan was to defeat President Donald Trump and not let him get reelected for four more years.

One of the major issues was policies and reform for police procedures due to all the shooting against Black African American people. Today my mind was on the two reasons why I would consider getting married at the age of fifty-eight: (1) children and (2) the sexual companionship and love. It would never be for money. I woke up this morning, sitting at the coffee shop, just talking with a couple of old school friends; the Caucasian guys were talking about the ups and downs that were going on in current society, with all the police race shooting and protest against racism in America. I came to find out something in history; I never knew that a Black man named John Henson was the president of the continental United States even before George Washington became the first president of the United State. Also a Black man by the name of Anthony Johnson owned Black slaves in the state of Virginia back in the 1800s. By listening to this information and confirming it, I was very surprised because we only heard about White people owning slaves back in these days. I could only figure the reason all negative comes out about slavery is because the people in government want to continue to cause conflict among all the races of people to stay divided and not be as one. I strongly feel that all history is good history and every side of the story needs to be told. Nevertheless, at the end of the day, we all as people, no matter what race, are victims of society and the daily events, problems that come with it. I truly feel we as people will have to follow man's laws and God's laws to survive and if we want to live a long life and become a law abiding citizen to be at peace. With what I have previously mentioned in my book, we as people have to deal year after year with all these nature of destruction, may it be hurricanes like Laura that just hit the southern course line near Texas and Louisiana. Out west in California, wild fires continued to destroy homes and communities and take human lives. Again, I say always remember this is God's world; we will just all be here until we expire.

The following are old sayings from the recovery I live by to reach this point in my life. Got more time than money. The best friend is always someone you don't know or just meant. Like Grandma said, "There is more than one fish in the sea." Nothing comes to a sleeper but a dream. A close mouth doesn't get fed. Thinking about life is like robbing Peter to pay Paul because Bill always wants his. The world will take from you when a person has nothing left to give but time. Another day, another dollar—you are going to spend a dollar or make dollar. Take a good look at ourselves. Talk to me with truth and no lies, which means be real. Live by the sawed, die by sawed, but if the sawed is just used, we will live to see another day. Fight for your life, either get busy living or get busy dying.

Chapter 4

Dealing with Death in My Life, Family, Friends, Mentors, and Icons We Have Lost

Today, I got a news that actor Chadwick Boseman died of a four-year battle with colon cancer at age forty-three. He starred in movies like Jackie Robinson, Thurgood Marshall, Black Panther, and more. Another icon legend, John Thompson, passed away the same week at age seventy-eight; he was known as Georgetown University head basketball coach who won three national championships.

On September 5, 2020, the Kentucky Derby was held on this day because of the health crisis that cancelled the event in May. Labor Day would be on Monday 2020, and all schools would be back in session on Tuesday, September 8, 2020, because of the national health crisis. My little brother's, Patrick, birthday was on September 11, 2020, and everything seemed to be doing okay at this point in his life. But we all know that every day is a new day, and we hope and pray for the best for all of mankind. This was the moment in my life when I was hoping to reach my goals and dreams to the very end. I turned 59 after a few months; God's been good. Keep hope alive and have faith; the journey is worth it. I was just thinking and writing about some of the thoughts in my mind because there is a big difference in being a boy to becoming a teenage young man and then becoming a full complete man who has to know wrongs from rights and learns self-discipline and responsibilities to deal with life challenges. Today is another day awake during the three S's—shit, shave, and shower—another one of my old saying. My writings are true, not fiction. I believe in my higher power and don't believe in make believe or dreams.

Today Dallas Cowboys played the Atlanta Falcons at noon. Sports was back for now at 50 percent capacity. My thoughts this morning was money. It's good to have money, but at the end of the day, there are certain things money can't just buy—to become young again when we get old. To give me my health from a terminal disease when I become ill. Time is almost up; I am just about at the end of the rainbow—another of my old sayings. NBA retired superstar, Michael Jordan, invested in NASCAR race team as the first majority Black owner. Another accomplished Black man, Deon Sanders, a retired NFL football star, became the head coach of Jackson State, a historical Black college football team. These were exciting great moments for African Americans in the year 2020 as time moved on for the next generation to begin their journey.

Today Chicago Bear running back Gale Sayers died at age seventy-seven; he was fighting the disease called dementia. Another famous African American, Bob Gibson, died because of pancreatic cancer at age eight-four; he was a famous baseball pitcher in the sixties and seventies for the St. Louis Cardinals. Also Johnnie Nash passed away on October 4, 2020 at age eighty; he was a well-known solo singer. I wrote and mentioned these important people because it was what I heard and had encountered daily during my lifetime and didn't want people to be forgotten for their great accomplishments to the world. It is very important that we know and value our past as we continue to live. I felt it important for the next generation to know the struggles that we as African Americans had to overcome, and it continued as I wrote my story today.

At this moment in my life, I am doing good. I have all the necessary things I need to live and would very much like to find another humble, kind, young woman before I go down this last path of my life. But I do know in the end, I can only enjoy life as it is while I am here and get things in order to leave the world behind.

On October 3, 2020, another police shooting occurred in a small town in Texas; thirty-one-year-old Johnathan Price was killed in Wolfe City, Texas. The incident was being investigated; a protest march was held, and the police officer had been arrested and charged with murder of an innocent citizen. The election for president of the United States was held on October 13, 2020, which was early voting. Election day was on November 3, 2020; this was to decide whether current president Donald Trump would be reelected for four more years. His opponent was Joe Biden and running mate, Kamala Harris.

I am feeling good about tomorrow, thinking positive, and continuing to stay involved in daily activities that I enjoy. I am looking forward to living a long peaceful life.

The news for today was hall fame second baseman Joe Morgan died at age seventy-seven; he played with the Cincinnati Reds. Major League Baseball Playoff started tonight in the new Global Life Park Stadium in Arlington, Texas; the National League Conference finals would be LA Dodgers and Atlanta Braves. There was another big event in the NBA Champion again since Coby Bryant led the team to the finals. Lebron James helped crown Los Angeles Lakers Champion of the 2020 season. Another important death this week was hall of fame San Francisco 49ers Fred Dean, who battled with cancer, died at age sixty-eight; he won two Super Bowls championships with the 49ers. Another great legend, Herb Adderley, a hall of fame cornerback who played for twelve years with the Green Bay Packers and Dallas Cowboys died on Friday at age eighty-one. Today, November 3, 2020, was the final day to vote for the president for the next four years. The final count would be in soon; the winner as of November 6, 2020, was Joe Biden and Kamala Harris with 270 electoral votes.

Today was my father's birthday; may he continue to be at peace. See you and mom soon.

Today the election results came in; Joe Biden and Kamala Harris had been elected as the forty-sixth president and vice president of the United States 2020. The inauguration was held on January 20, 2021. Markus Paul passed away because of health reasons. He was Dallas Cowboys' training coach who played defense back for six seasons with Chicago Bears and New England Patriots. He earned five Super Bowl rings at age fifty-four.

An African town located in Alabama where some of the first slaves were brought from West Africa to the United States in the 1860s was sold to slave owners. The history was unknown to me as of today; slaves arrived on the ship sake in the Niger river. The goal was to preserve the ship and its contents and rebuild the community of African town in Alabama.

On December 8, 2020, the first vaccine was issued in the United Kingdom in London to a ninety-one-year-old woman. The vaccine should be given to the United States next week before Christmas. It was always an opposite to every situation or solution that existed in life. This might be what we call choices or whatever road we choose to take.

On December 12, 2020, I got a news that Charlie Pride died at age eight-six because of complications of coronavirus. He was a popular country singer. On December 20, 2020, it was just about to be New Years. The real-life Joe Clark, who played the principal in the movie *Lean On Me*, starring actor Morgan Freedman who helped kids become better students, passed away at age eight-two. Also Dr. Dennis Dunkin died at age eighty because of COVID-19 complication. He was a very important educator in the Fort Worth Independent School System. Also Floyd Little hall fame running back for the Denver Broncos died of brain cancer at age seventy-eight on New Year's Day 2021.

On December 14, 2020, the first shots of the vaccine were given to frontline workers. It was Christmas Eve and 350,000 people died because of coronavirus. I continued to try to end my journey in this book, but more and more important influencers in everyday life continued to pass away who need not to be forgotten in American history. The next entry to my final chapter would be January 1, 2021. The New Year was here; no regrets if things didn't turn out like I would like. It has been a good journey no matter what the year 2021 has to offer.

On January 22, 2021, the legend baseball player, Hank Aaron, passed away at age eight-six; he held the league record for home runs at 755 for thirty years with Atlanta Braves. Also the great actress, Cicely Tyson, passed away at age ninety-six; these legends should never be forgotten for their great accomplishments in American society. Kenny Washington was one of the first Black NFL football players who was allowed to sign a contract to play in the league for the Los Angeles Rams in the year 1945. The league was established in 1920, when only a few Blacks were allowed to play until completely cut out. The year 1945 bought about a complete change for Black players.

On February 7, 2021, Super Bowl LV was being played in Tampa, Florida; the teams playing were the Kansas City Chiefs vs. the Tampa Bay Buccaneers. Today another legend, Leon Spinks, who defeated Muhammad Ali for the heavyweight boxing championship belt in 1978, passed away. Leon suffered with prostate cancer; he was sixty-seven years old.

On February 8, 2021, Tom Brady became the oldest quarterback at age forty-two; he won eight super bowl championships—Tampa Bay, 31; Kansas City Chiefs, 9.

On February 22, 2021, the snowstorm was over; it lasted for about a week, totaling 139 hours accidents, water line frozen; electricity power shut down for most homes for about a week, causing people many problems. Coronavirus has killed about 500,000 people as of today. Life is full of new challenges in these times and days we live. Today I got a news that an old friend and classmate from the sixth grade had passed away; William Mookie was an excellent person and student athlete. God bless and I will see you and others soon. Also Veron Jordan died at age eight-five; he was a well-known civil rights leader in Washington. Another important person who continues to live as of today is Darren Walker; he is the president of Ford Motor Companies in New York City. He continues to give back to unfortunate people. Also I got news today that the famous actor and rapper, Earl Simmons, known as DMX, passed away at age fifty because of drug overdose in New York City. Michael K. Williams died at age fifty-four-years-old in New York City. He was known as an actor in the series *The Wire* and other movies. He should never be forgotten. Today news was that Colin Powell, secretary of state, died at age eighty-four. He was the first African American to hold the position. He should never be forgotten. Today Paul Mooney, comedian/writer, died at age seventy-nine. He should never be forgotten.

On April 21, 2021, another close and good friend from the old neighborhood, Arthur Ray Shannon, passed away at age sixty. Today is September 25, 2021, Saturday, and I got news that Janell Box Nash passed away because of coronavirus symptoms that has taken so many lives. She was my sister-in-law; my little brother, Anthony's, wife for thirty years. Today is September 30, 2021, and a few weeks later, I got news that a close neighbor in my old neighborhood, Rose Canady, passed away, Troy Canady's mother. A very nice person and friend should never be forgotten. We live life daily after birth, not knowing if we are going to survive the challenges that life has to offer. As teenagers on the way to becoming young men, we are born to die; we don't know from day to day if we will reach the age of twenty, thirty, forty, or fifty and if this is going to be our last day on earth. So it is very important for us people to get busy living because every day is a conscious choice; we have to make decisions on what path is best for us.

The book is an inspiration about the life of a Black man's poetry and thoughts of depression on how life should be at the age sixty. The book was inspired do to overcoming my learning disabilities, drug addiction, and poor relationships throughout my life. Always think positively; it's not over until it's over. Everything seems to be repeating itself as life goes forward. The younger people are getting older; the older people are dying. My life should have been over already before I wrote this book. But with God's will and having faith in him, I am still here. Life is good at this point. There are no guarantees that life is going to be the way we want it. Life is about giving it a try and a chance to become someone. Another true saying in life is we all have to know when to get off the boat because at some point, it could sink. We all have to believe there is something or someone we are willing to die for. We get old; we get sick. We can be taking down the wrong path. At the end of the day, we just need to believe in God. What death means to me personally will be the end of a journey of experiences, having faith, disappointments, struggles, learning, and realization of knowing there is a conclusion to life as we know it. My life was a good one and I have no regrets about anything. We as individuals have to take the good with the bad things that we encounter along the way. We can't go backward; we can only move forward and become a better person at whatever we choose to pursue in life. I've never been afraid of dying as a young person. I always had a thirst for living. I know I will be going home soon to be with my mother and father again, and I am ready. Today, got news on November 15, 2021, Monday evening. Aunt Daisy passed away at age eighty-one. She was a strong, kind, and fun person and should never be forgotten. Also I would like to mention my uncle Daniel has recently passed on January 30, 2022 he was 78 years old. The world is a beautiful place; to all the young generation, enjoy life and don't give up on yourself no matter how bad things maybe. Whoever reads this book should be motivated, have encouragement, hope, faith for success to become whoever you want to become in life. God forgives me for all the things I left undone or did not finish during my journey. The word *power* to me means a peace of mind, knowledge about what you, as a person, can achieve, and money as I live my last years. Briefly meant Timothy Lane author of the book *Trapped inside My Mind*.

Today is October 1, 2021, and these are the lists of relatives, in-laws, and family members who continue to live today: Kenneth and Sharon Nash, Anthony and Janell Nash, Patrick and Melody Nash, Cassandra Ates Nash, Valencia and Melvin McShann. The kids and young adults are Megan, Lemarcus, Xavier, Daisha Madeline, McKenna, Kawana, Daytron. Uncles who continue to live as of today are Daniel W., Charles W., and Rufus W. Aunts who are currently living as of today are Margie, Themla, Mattie, Margene, Ruth, Vera. Cousins who continue to live as of today are Gerald, Ann, Cynthia, Debra, Jackie W., Jackie D., Vantrice W., Brandon, Tomekia, Kevin N., Michelle N., Russell N., Michelle B., Sherrie B., Lasalle Jr., Carolyn, Janice W., Arthur Jr., Daniel Jr. Tanita, Timothy W., Christopher L., Kareem L., Harold Jr., Deon W., Gratis Jr., Raymond Jr., Terry W., David A., Shirley A., Ester A., Rita E., Chili E., Charles Jr. W., Roger M., Austin M., Shelia M., Mandy C., Troy

C., Bennie N., Themla N., Raymond N., Rosalette W., kershala W., Ingrid W., Kevin W., Derrick W., Johnny W., Xavier F., Melvin Jr., Marvin B., and Charlotte B.

Got news. Cousin Gerald Woolen passed away on March 2, 2023. He had health problems with COPD lung disease. He was Aunt Dorothy Marie's son, and his sister's name is Jackie. Gerald was a good cousin, a military army, and a hard-working honorable person. We live like a man. We die like a man. Nobody knows God's plan, but God has a plan for everyone. I have enjoyed the pleasure of learning and embracing the kindness and love of family members who have recently passed on and will see them soon. Rest in peace my cousin, uncles, aunties, and in-laws.

Lance Reddick died at sixty on March 17, 2023. He starred in roles and series such as *The Wire*, *John Wick*, series *Bosch*, *New York Undercover*, and movie *White House Down*. Born June 7, 1962, in Baltimore, Maryland.

Today's news, on March 21, 2023, Willis Reed died at age eighty. One of the best basketball players of all time. Played with the New York Knicks. These people should never be forgotten for their contribution to life. The old saying goes, "Don't put too much heat under the pan because it just might boil over." We all make conscious choices in life, good or bad.

Today is March 24, 2023. News of a young Hispanic woman, thirty years old, lost her life in a road rage shooting in the East Dallas area for no apparent reason. Just another sign of times we are living each and every day.

Today is March 25, 2023. Another natural disaster, a tornado, has hit Rolling Fork, Mississippi, killing twenty people. Also, another tornado hit Wynne, Arkansas. Death toll was thirty-two lives lost.

Today is March 30, 2023. Today I truly believe in restoration as I believe in God as my higher power and savior. As I breathe today as a human being. We as African American people should be repaid for the wrongs; stolen ownership of land, homes, and property; and the inhumane conditions as human beings in the past living conditions we had to encounter.

Today is March 31, 2023. Two things in this world people crave most are attention and control. If we can't have these feelings, we feel lost are unwanted. It's not the color of your skin; to me it's what can you do for me or each other today.

These are my theories of life and the people whom we deal with daily. We as people all have feelings we have to control are deal with daily, no matter what color of our skin. Here are a few more good books to enjoy while living life: *Love Outside the Lines* by Pastor Jimmy Rollins. Another excellent book to read while waiting on a better day: *Don't Let Them Bury My Story*, written by author Viola Ford Fletchers, 109 years old, the oldest living survivor of the Greenwood Massacre.

Today is May 6, 2023. We have experienced another mass shooting in Allen, Texas, outside a mall outlet. Eight people killed, five injured. A sign of violence on innocent people minding their own business shopping.

Today May 13, 2023, learned in a movie called *Sweetwater*, professional basketball team called the Harlem Globetrotters in the 1950s was the first Black basketball team. Sweetwater became one of three Black players to enter the National Basketball Association. This opened the doors for all majority players today. Also news of today, the Denver Nuggets versus the Miami Heat for the NBA Championship game. Denver wins 94–89, a 4–1 seven-game series.

Today is May 19, 2023. Jim Brown passed at age eighty-seven. He was a professional football player and actor for many years. He will be greatly missed and should never be forgotten.

Today is May 24, 2023. Another icon has passed: Tina Turner, born Anna Mae Bullock on November 26, 1939, in Nutbush, Tennessee. She was known as the queen of rock and roll. She was eighty-three years old. She should never be forgotten. Also, another great actor and icon has passed, John Beasley, at the age of seventy-nine years old. He played in the movies *Everwood*, *The Soul Man*, also films named *Rudy*, *Walking Tall*, and *The Mighty Ducks*.

Today, June 10, 2023, just waking on Sunday morning, thinking about who am I and what have I accomplished in my life. It is a big difference between worrying about dying and thinking about dying. Some people don't want to follow, and some people don't want to lead. But in the end, we can only look at ourselves in the mirror. Words from a wise man: "I not trying to choose a dream. I am trying to achieve my dream."

Chapter 5

Enjoying the final days of my life at age sixty

The last five years every man for himself, God for us all. The purpose of these thoughts at age sixty is the body and mind feels different as time goes on living out the aches, pain, and grief of a more mature person. The purpose as people, we are not perfect, we will make mistakes alone the way during our lifetime. The message is to keep faith in God Jesus Christ. The verse purpose 8:28 Romans and we know that all things work together for good to them that love God, to them who are the called according to his purpose. It seems like the world try too through you away. But the challenge is to continue to care for yourself and be the person you are willing to be. Design a plan for short term and long-term goals. Nothing is full proof but can be accomplished with time. I never believed in plans before reaching this age, but as the years went by come to find out thinking ahead can pay-off in the long run. Staying aware is like staying alive. Full steam ahead at the end of the day it is all about happiness and getting the honors we deserve. Today I awake feeling tired of all the unnecessary killing among African Americans people. The young generation hating against one another. This is called Black on Black crime. I say am blessed and thankful to my God. Corinthians 1 verse 15:57 But thanks be to God, which giveth us the victory through our Lord Jesus Christ. I am enjoying the last years in peace. This is a fact not fiction. In today's world as I continue to live, we eat food that turns into maggots are mold. An excellent habit to start early in life is to eat fruit, vegetables, Lean portions of protein. Better yet no meat diet and try fastening a day are two. Maintaining your bodies intake. We continue shooting each other just driving to work just to make a living. This is what they call road rage senseless anger. The year December 2019 world changed the lights went out. The coronavirus had arrived in the United States and killed millions of people and the virus is under control, but still exist as of today. Today is January 16, 2023, the world revolves changing decade after decade. Year after year, meeting and engaging in different relationships with different friends, people we meet daily, people we grow up with until the end of life. My concerns today is with the 3H's Health, Happiness, and Home as I live out the last years of my life. Today got news Mrs. Box had passed at age 88, she was Janell's mother. We all will meet our demise one day, it is just a matter of When, Where, and How. My theory is you always get better response spreading more with honey than spreading mess. We must carve out our own way in life and the way you think. This way you have only yourself to blame. Today is a new day, and new year 2023. It is such thing as a higher power, a higher love. Not just unconditional love are relationship type of love. Am talking about the love of internal love, salvation for the love of our lord Jesus Christ our savior. Today is January 9, 2023, the college national championship game Texas Christian University verse University Georgia for the best college football team of 2022. Finial score Georgia Bulls dogs 65, TCU Horn frogs 7. Would like to give a kind prayer, shutout to those brothers and sisters from the old neighborhood who I grew up with doing my journey. These people have been deceased for some time by name Richard W, Michael R, L.C. Sullivan, Dottie S, Betty C, Larry R, Gary T, Ray Shannon, Herman G, Dwayne F, Ly dell F, Clifford S, Sandy C, Michael P. This is what remembrance verse 1:3 Timothy I thank God, whom I serve from my forefathers with pure conscience, that without ceasing I have remembrance of thee in my prayer's night and day. News of today franco Harris passed away one of the greatest running backs ever played in the NFL history dies at 72. Hopeful in these final days, I can be more about the Holy Bible the real book of life. So far it has gotten me to this point in my life. Corinthians 2 verse 5:7 for we walk by faith, not by sight. Not totally been aware God does really exist. And presently becoming aware it's time to stop living such a foolish life. Knowing God will forgive and take care of people who walk in the darkness about his faith doing wrong evil and sinful things. Book verse 22:19 Revelation, and if any man shall take away from the words of the book of this prophecy, God shall take away his part out of the book of life, and out of the holy city, and from the things which are written in this book. I recall time in my life, I was not a wise man. I would indulge doing wrongs things using drugs, taking things that don't belong to me. I feel grateful today I have been able to become a wiser man at age sixty. Asking God to forgive me for all the sinful wrongs, I have done in my life. Wise proverbs verse 1:5, A wise man will hear, and will increase learning, and a man of understanding shall attain unto wise counsel and become a better person. These are my finial days, I would like to travel, spend time in peace, walk-in faith, seek out god's word, give God my time. Hebrews verse 11:13, These all died in faith, not having received the promises, but having seen them a far off, and were persuaded of them, and embraced them, and confessed that they were strangers and pilgrims on the earth. Hebrews Verse 11:1, now faith is the substance of things hoped for, the evidence of things not seen. It is my time to be at peace with God. Ecclesiastes verse 3:8 A time to love, and a time to hate, a time of war, and a time of peace. I will always make time to love the beautiful things the world and what life has to offer. Whether it be people, material objects, Lust, money, successful career. Like I mentioned in my early Chapters, God forgive me for the things I could not get done, while my presents here on earth. Thanks for all the accomplishments, good times, and friends, I encounter alone the way. My journey is with you God, Corinthians 1 verse 15:57, but thanks be to God, which giveth us the victory through our Lord Jesus Christ. You as God have had mercy, love, trust, grace, hope and faith in me as a human being. Ephesians verse 5:20, Giving thanks always for all things unto God and the father in the name of our Lord Jesus Christ. Got news today January 15,2023 another relative past Uncle Jimmy De shone, from Tulsa Oklahoma heart attack was cause of death rest in peace. Today is

January 16,2023 Martin Luther King Jr. federal Holiday. Today my sister Valencia will be sworn in for a 5th term at South Dallas Government Center as Justice of the peace court judge. I have learned to live day by day, seven days in a week, four weeks in a month, 365 days in a year, 12 months. Life continues to be the same if you are not motivated to making progress. We as people must seek some form of Love and Happiness. Matthew verse 7:7 ask, and it shall be given, you seek, and ye shall find, knock and it shall be opened unto you. Today Dallas Cowboys win their first- round playoff game in 30 years. Finial score Dallas 31, Tampa Bay 14. The two teams that made it to final game super bowl 57, 2023 were the Kansas City Chiefs versus Philadelphia Eagles final score Chiefs 38 Eagles 35. Life continues to be a challenge daily, one day at a time is how I approach life at this age. It is easier for me this way. A good book about a young boy with autism, Title All roads Lead to Love, author Dr. Rhonda Brown Crowder. Excellent reading while relaxing waiting for a better day. Bessie Coleman was first female African American pilot to hold license on June 15, 1921. She was Born in Atlanta Texas. We as people must find ways to reach our goals. Many people lose their focus on how to live life. I just wanted to encourage people young and old. Challenge yourselves don't give up. Many people get depressed, commit suicide, loss mental control hurt themselves and others. This is not what God wants, John 1 verse 4.7 Love one another, beloved, let us love one another, for love is of God, and everyone that loveth is born of God, and know eth God. The world is a place where there are laws. There are more good people than bad people. It is made and design of state and federal government. We as people have the right to choose whatever party of government we wish to represent. We pay tax on our homes and earnings. We live in a structured society with rules, laws, and regulations to follow. Today is February 8, 2023, on this day another world disaster earthquake has happen in the country of Turkey and northwest Syria killing as many today 40,000 thousand people including children. God has a plan for everybody, live your life with grace, love, hope. Because the end is sure to come. There are different types of religions the most common to me are the Baptist faith. They believe in being emerge into holy water to become member. Baptists have strong strict Christian belief in God Jesus Christ. Methodist belief is humanity and salvation for all. Methodists believe there is a God of love. Do no harm, do good. We must pay for our learning in life whether good are bad. We do not have very much control as humans that is why, I strongly believe this is Gods world. We are only here for a short time to make our existence known. We must teach our youth generation how to choose the righteous path to become successful. Live like a man, die like a man. John verse 17:4, I have glorified thee on the earth, I have finished the work which thou gavesth me to do. Like, I have said before, many good people have pasted on, we must know as mature adults when our time is finished. Timothy 2 verse 4:7, I have fought a good fight, I have finished my course, I have kept the faith.

The End.

About the Author

Gary J. Nash is a fifty-nine-year-old African American who was raised in the Dallas-Fort Worth Metropolitan Area. He is currently single and has no children. He earned his high school diploma from Wilmer-Hutchins High School. Also, he attended University of North Texas and earned a degree in rehabilitation studies. One of his goals during his youth was to become a homeowner. He also had some military experience with the US Air Force Reserve. Having parents who were educators in the Dallas school district, he tried that much harder to complete his goals. The strict upbringing pressured him to complete some form of education; he worked hard at becoming a better learner and listener so as he got older he would be able to accomplish his goals and feel part of the world. It took some work and help from his friends and family. But today he stands alone going through life's daily cycles of surviving ups and downs. Education was always important in his upbringing, but he was just not that good at paying attention. He could have stopped trying, but he didn't, and by the will and the word of his higher power, he completed some of his personal goals. This is what he calls a foundation. At the end of day, with this being said, life is not over yet. He will be sixty years old in November 2022.

www.ingramcontent.com/pod-product-compliance
Lightning Source LLC
LaVergne TN
LVHW041628070726
842790LV00009B/190